A Surprising God

D1408844

A Surprising God

Advent Devotions
for an Uncertain Time

Thomas G. Long and
Donyelle C. McCray

WESTMINSTER
JOHN KNOX PRESS
LOUISVILLE • KENTUCKY

First edition
Published by Westminster John Knox Press
Louisville, Kentucky

21 22 23 24 25 26 27 28 29 30—10 9 8 7 6 5 4 3 2 1

Book design by Sharon Adams
Cover design by designpointinc.com
Cover art: Be Thou My Vision *by Mike Moyers. Used by permission:*

Library of Congress Cataloging-in-Publication Data

Names: Long, Thomas G., 1946- author. | McCray, Donyelle C., author.
Title: A surprising God : Advent devotions for an uncertain time / Thomas
   G. Long and Donyelle C. McCray.
Description: First edition. | Louisville, Kentucky : Westminster John Knox
   Press, 2021. | Summary: "Mindful of the stresses of life today, Thomas
   G. Long and Donyelle C. McCray offer daily devotions for Advent and
   Christmas that invite readers to honest reflection on the challenges of
   being people of faith in this moment"-- Provided by publisher.
Identifiers: LCCN 2021026165 (print) | LCCN 2021026166 (ebook) | ISBN
   9780664267230 (paperback) | ISBN 9781646982158 (ebook)
Subjects: LCSH: Advent--Prayers and devotions. | LCGFT: Devotional
   literature.
Classification: LCC BV40 .L664 2021 (print) | LCC BV40 (ebook) | DDC
   242/.33--dc23
LC record available at https://lccn.loc.gov/2021026165
LC ebook record available at https://lccn.loc.gov/2021026166

Most Westminster John Knox Press books are available at special quantity discounts when purchased in bulk by corporations, organizations, and special-interest groups. For more information, please e-mail SpecialSales@wjkbooks.com.

Contents

Preface

In a fine essay, Old Testament scholar Walter Brueggemann once contrasted the work of two of his colleagues.
The first scholar, he said, sees the Old Testament as a
collection of books that emerged out of vigorous fights
over ideas and influence. The Old Testament, this
scholar maintained, arose from a tug-of-war of compet-
ing ideologies and sources of power. By contrast, the
second scholar, while certainly aware of the social forces
at work in the Old Testament, seeks to discover a cohe-
sive voice resounding in the deep recesses of the texts,
one that speaks across the ages and beyond the clash of
immediate social struggle. At first, these two vastly different approaches seem to move in opposite directions, said
Brueggemann, but actually they complement each other,
and both are needed. The first, he said, seeks to hear the
Bible *in the fray*, while the second seeks to hear Scripture
above the fray.[1]

That combination of "in the fray" and "above the fray"
could well describe the Advent devotions in this volume.

We wrote them in and for this volatile moment in history, when all of us are very much aware of how deeply in the fray we are. The ravages of a tragic pandemic that has taken the lives of millions of people around the world, the pressure cooker of politics threatening to tear our society apart, the fragile economy that manages to exacerbate the already painful division between the haves and the have-nots, the racial tensions among us that have become all the more apparent by recent events, the loneliness and isolation of so many—these are the frayed conditions in which we all live and in which we sought to see Advent signs of God's surprising appearing. But we were also straining to listen above the fray for the familiar and trusted promises of God, a God who "advents" into our lives in every season of history and whose love endures forever.

The devotions here are alert to a constant theme of the Advent season: waiting patiently in hope for the coming of God. But they are written for a time when patience can be worn thin, when holding onto hope is challenging, and when the peace and joy of the promised Christ child can feel elusive. We feel kinship with the psalmist, who cries out in distress,

> My soul thirsts for God,
>   for the living God.
> When shall I come and behold
>   the face of God?
> My tears have been my food
>   day and night,
> while people say to me continually,
>   "Where is your God?"
>
> (Ps. 42:2–3)

In this time of thirsting for God, we cling in faith to the God who surprises by providing refreshing springs in the driest of places and who allows light to break into our world in the bleakest of times.

There are twenty-eight devotions included in this volume, one for each of the days in Advent. Half of them were written by Donyelle, who teaches preaching and Christian spirituality at Yale Divinity School. She has a deep interest in the history and practice of African American preaching, and she has written a book on Julian of Norwich, whose life of devotion was itself a sermon. The other half were written by Tom, who is an emeritus professor of preaching at Emory University's Candler School of Theology. Tom has worked extensively in the area of biblical interpretation in sermons and has written commentaries on Matthew, Hebrews, and the Pastoral Epistles.

For the First Week of Advent, Tom wrote the devotions for Days 1, 3, 5, and 7, and Donyelle for Days 2, 4, and 6. For the Second Week of Advent, Donyelle wrote Days 1, 3, 5, and 7, and Tom for Days 2, 4, and 6. For the Third Week of Advent, Tom wrote for Days 1, 3, 5, and 7, and Donyelle for Days 2, 4, and 6. For the Fourth Week of Advent, Donyelle wrote Days 1, 3, 5, and 7, and Tom for Days 2, 4, and 6.

For each day in Advent, we selected one of the Scripture passages for that day in the Revised Common Lectionary and allowed that passage to set the tone for the devotion. As an additional resource in reflecting on the motifs of Advent, each devotion is accompanied by a brief prayer connected to the theme of the devotion. Writing these devotions was, for both of us, an exercise in deepening our own faith. In myriad ways, the events of the past year have shown us that we can be surprised by pain and sorrow, but we have also come to see how much we can be surprised by God's grace. It is our hope that readers will likewise be strengthened in the Advent season in their quest for God.

Donyelle C. McCray, Yale Divinity School
Thomas G. Long, Candler School of Theology
Epiphany 2021

First Week of Advent

The God of Surprises

Luke 21:25–36

> Now when these things begin to take place, stand
> up and raise your heads, because your redemp-
> tion is drawing near.
>
> —Luke 21:28

The Kentucky poet and farmer Wendell Berry is a well-
known agrarian and fierce advocate of small towns, family
farms, and loving care of the land. He is also, curiously,
an opponent of all attempts to predict the future. Regard-
ing the idea of the future, he says, "I won't grant it much
standing," and, as for predicting the future, "I won't grant
it much respect."[1]

Why? Don't we depend upon predictions of the
future? Who would know whether to take an umbrella
to work were it not for experts forecasting the weather?
How would we know whether to buy a Honda or a Ford
if the consumer magazines didn't provide predictions of
reliability? How could economists do their work without
prognoses of the markets? What would cable TV discuss
were there no political polls?

For Berry, though, since we cannot really know the future, shrouded as it is in mystery, all predictions are merely projections cantilevered from the past, guesses cast forward from what we already know and have experienced. What is more, the motives underlying predictions are suspect, reflecting a deep hunger to protect ourselves from the unknown, to exert ultimate control over life, to eliminate all unpredictability and surprise.

Those who are familiar with Scripture will recognize that yearning for a future free from surprises is, down deep, actually a desire to be free of God. If our predicting the future is really only a projection of what we already know and who we already are, then we are imagining a future inhabited only by our powers and desires, one that we humans can dominate and control. But the living God seen in the Bible is a God full of surprises, one who since Eden has frustrated all human efforts to eliminate unpredictability. "Do not remember the former things," God says. "I am about to do a new thing" (Isa. 43:18–19).

This surprising God is at the heart of Advent. Like waves breaking on the beach, God keeps "adventing" into our lives in ways that always amaze. Who could have predicted the creation itself? It was a gift that arose *ex nihilo*, a surprising act of grace that God performed simply for the love of it. What forecaster could have foretold that the Red Sea would have parted for the children of Israel just as the Egyptian war chariots were closing in for the kill? What about those wise men from the East? For all their horoscopes and charts, the new king of the Jews did not turn out to be a ruler in Jerusalem's royal palace as they had predicted, but a humble child found in little Bethlehem in the arms of his mother. And not even the disciples were prepared for the great Easter surprise: an empty tomb and a risen Savior.

What about the ultimate future? In Luke, Jesus tells us there will be future wars, earthquakes, famines, and plagues. Well, knowing history, we could have predicted that. But then he tells us that at the end of all things there is a surprise. Don't look down, Jesus says. Look up, and you "will see 'the Son of Man coming in a cloud' with power and great glory. . . . Stand up and raise your heads, because your redemption is drawing near" (Luke 21:27–28).

Who could have imagined *that*? Only Jesus, the one who has come, is with us now, and is Lord even of the surprising future.

Prayer for the Day

O God, you come to us in ways we could never have expected or imagined. Do not let us become so complacent, so ready to manage the reality of our lives, that we miss the surprises of grace and redemption that you bring to us. We pray in the name of Jesus Christ, our Peace. Amen.

Do You Understand?

2 Peter 3:1–18

But do not ignore this one fact, beloved, that
with the Lord one day is like a thousand years,
and a thousand years are like one day.
							—2 Peter 3:8

One of the most vexing lessons uncertainty teaches us is
that we do not control time. Rarely do we have even the
slightest understanding of it. We only swim in the sea of
time and feel ourselves either carried by its mysterious
current or adrift in its slow, ambiguous drag.

During a visit to an Episcopal church some time ago,
I stood next to the priest, John, and shook hands with
members of the congregation as they filed out. Since
many of the members were from Nigeria, or Ghana, or,
like John, from Liberia, these greetings took a while.
John asked about extended family members, about children's progress in school, about sports and recipes. All
the while one of the younger members—he couldn't
have been more than three years old—waved excitedly at

John while he waited for his turn. His eyes were fixed on John's colorfully embroidered robes and biretta. When the youngster's family finally reached us in line, he reached out to embrace John and began to shout, "Hi, God! Hi, God! Hiiiiiiiii!" John let the boy play with his chasuble and stole, and then looked into his eyes as he explained that he was not God, that he was a priest who helped everybody worship God, that God was invisible and everywhere, everlasting, and would always be with him. "Do you understand?" When the child nodded and smiled, John placed him in his father's arms and waved as the family headed to the door. Just as they entered the doorway, the boy turned back and waved, "Bye, God!"

Because we can only partially comprehend divinity, we are given glimpses in kind-eyed humans who radiate God's grace. Because we are creatures of time who appear as mists and then vanish (Jas. 4:14), we need metaphors to understand God's timing. "Peter" (whether the apostle, his deputy, or successor) provides one when he explains that "with the Lord one day is like a thousand years, and a thousand years are like one day." And, after offering this bite-sized explanation, he turns to us like my friend, John, to ask if we understand. How can we? Yet, Peter compels us to stretch our imaginations and try as best we can to think in eons.

As urgent as they may feel, our doubts and uncertainties are seen clearest through the frame of eternity. Many of the things that consume our schedules and seem to define our lives will pass away. The temporal will yield to the eternal and do so with a clap (2 Pet. 3:10)! This means the jobs and all of the worries about work; the plans; the material objects that surround us from day to day—the sofas and comforters and lamps; but also organizing concepts like nation-states, land borders, age, race, gender. In other words, most of what structures human life and shapes identity.

Peter points to an invisible reality that we can only barely fathom now. How the veil separating the temporal and eternal will lift we can't know. But the knowledge of God's eternity and our finitude casts a clarifying light on our daily decisions. We can more readily discern what matters. Perhaps we are gentler toward the earth and to each person God puts before us. And surely the daily struggles of our lives have a bit more context. Our small increments of time are long enough for loving action and long enough to reveal the endless grace of the Everlasting One who alone gives our fleeting lives meaning. It helps to lift our pressing worries to heaven. The God who holds eternity can be trusted with the next twenty-four hours, whatever they hold.

Prayer for the Day

In a world that is passing away, your love, O Lord, is our one true anchor. Put our momentary troubles in perspective. Give us today that supernatural peace that flows from the world that is to come. Amen.

The Bright Morning Star

Revelation 22:12–16

> I am the Alpha and the Omega, the first and the last, the beginning and the end.
> —Revelation 22:13

"We Shall Overcome" was the anthem of the 1960s' civil rights movement, but the song was more than merely the rallying cry of a political movement. It was a gospel hymn of hope. The chorus—"O, deep in my heart I do believe we shall overcome someday"—is rooted in the Christian conviction that history is not "a tale told by an idiot" but is, instead, the canvas upon which Christ is painting a future of peace and justice.

When "We Shall Overcome" was sung in 1965 during the days of the march from Selma to Montgomery, the stanzas were punctuated by shouts of "My Lord!" John Lewis, who was one of the leaders of that march, said of the song, "It gave you a sense of faith, a sense of strength, to continue to struggle, to continue to push on. And you would lose your sense of fear. You were prepared to march into hell's fire."[2]

The book of Revelation knows of hope, but it is also brutally honest about the cruelties and injustices of human society. Human experience is blood-soaked, filled with suffering and death. But Revelation proclaims that history is not moving toward oblivion but toward Christ, who is Alpha and Omega, the beginning of all things and also the end of all things. One day, Revelation sings, God will wipe away every tear, and death, mourning, crying, and pain will be no more (Rev. 21:4). As the priest in Bernanos's *Diary of a Country Priest*, who is deeply alert to the sufferings of his flock, affirms, "And I feel that such distress, distress that has forgotten even its name, that has ceased to reason or to hope, that lays its tortured head at random, will awaken one day on the shoulder of Jesus Christ."[3]

But Revelation does more than ask us to rest our hope on some distant horizon. Yes, the Christ who is Alpha and Omega, who was there at the creation of the world, will also be there at the end to receive the world into his arms of mercy and love, but Christ is also among us now. "I am . . . the bright morning star," Christ proclaims at the end of the book of Revelation (22:16).

The morning star blazes in the darkness of the eastern sky just before dawn, announcing that the rising of the sun is near. Just so, even as we wait for the dawning of God's new day, the light of Christ breaks even into the present darkness.

For all who wait in the long and anguished night comforting a feverish child, or who are sleepless because of grief or pain, or who feel anxious over a broken relationship, or who are searching for justice long delayed, Christ does not leave us abandoned. He comes to us with wings of mercy and healing. He touches our troubled brow with compassion. He shines forth in the deepest darkness. He is the bright morning star in the middle of the night, proclaiming that the light of dawn is near.

"O, deep in my heart I do believe . . ."

Prayer for the Day

O God of Mercy, it is difficult to wait in the darkness, not knowing how or when our fears and anxieties will subside. Send to us in the gloom of night the bright Morning Star, who brings comfort and hope and who announces the sure promise of your new day. Come, Lord Jesus! Amen.

Discerning the Signs

Luke 11:29–32

"See, something greater than Jonah is here!"
—Luke 11:32b

Isn't it natural to want a sign? To want some indication that as we make our way through the dark, we are on the right path? Thankfully, God has a long history of giving signs like love tokens. Each sign is unique to the person who needs it. Abraham's anguish is soothed by a canopy of twinkling stars that assure him of descendants. Moses gets a burning bush, plus ten plagues to dole out to the pharaoh. Gideon gets a wet fleece, and when that sign isn't enough, he gets a dry one. Mary gets a whole conversation with the angel Gabriel. As it turns out, these signs were necessary because each person faced a monumental challenge. Signs equipped our spiritual ancestors to take the next step forward into a veiled future.

But the trouble with signs is that they are easily misread or only understood in hindsight. Harriet Powers, a nineteenth-century African American quilter, took an unusual approach in one of her quilts. She depicted biblical scenes in which divine signs were misinterpreted or ignored: Noah's neighbors scoff at him instead of joining him in the ark, Jonah refuses the assignment in Nineveh and finds himself in the belly of a whale, and a heavenly dove descends on Christ—a sign humanity flouts in the crucifixion.[4] And maybe to show that the pattern of misreading signs continues centuries later, Powers included additional quilt panels that recount scenes from more recent history. These include atmospheric events that were believed to indicate divine judgment, like the eerie darkness that persisted throughout the day on May 19, 1780 (later attributed to pollution) and a meteor shower that prompted waves of terror in 1846. She also dedicated a quilt panel to November 13, 1833, a night when falling stars dotted the horizon. Maybe God hoped a sky full of falling stars would inspire awe, but cows and horses screamed in terror, birds screeched, and dogs panicked and ran in circles. And humans? They thought the world was coming to an end. Rather than a moment of beauty, the falling stars were interpreted as a sign of judgment. All in all, Powers's quilt suggests that as miraculous as signs are, they come with the responsibility of faithful response. Eventually, the time for seeking signs expires, and the time comes to act on the signs we've been given.

Jesus alludes to such a moment when he says, "'This generation is an evil generation; it asks for a sign, but no sign will be given to it except the sign of Jonah'" (Luke 11:29). We have been given the sign of all signs in Christ. This sign is more than the cross—crucial though it is—but the whole life of Jesus—his pattern of feasting, blessing, healing, and withdrawing to pray. We have been given his model of surrendering, dying, and rising in glory. Hour by hour, the Spirit bears us up, offering tender reminders of Christ's presence. Since our lives are lived in the presence and power of Jesus, our call now is not to seek signs, but to become signs—to move through the world as signs of his joy, mediators of his compassion and justice. We are harbingers of the end of the present age and signs of the new world that is to come.

Prayer for the Day

Merciful God, you are always and everywhere bringing life out of death. Make us unmistakable signs of your grace in the world, bearers of your light to those who need it most. Amen.

Living and Dying in Christ

Philippians 1:12–21

For to me, living is Christ and dying is gain.
—Philippians 1:21

Just days before he was executed in a Nazi prison, the courageous German theologian and pastor Dietrich Bonhoeffer penned a poem titled "Who Am I?"[5] In the poem, Bonhoeffer wondered about his true identity, who he really was beneath appearances, beneath even his own secret fears. Was he the calm, cheerful person of faith that some saw in him, a man who bore his imprisonment with a smile and an air of proud confidence? Or was he the lonely and restless prisoner that he secretly felt himself to be, a man trapped like a bird in a cage, a man for whom prayer seemed empty and for whom life had sunk into despair? "Who am I?" Bonhoeffer wondered.

It is a question that each of us must face. Who are we? Who are we really? There are, of course, the easy self-descriptions we use when meeting people for the first time: "Hi, I'm Rachael from Des Moines. I'm married to Andy, and we have two children. I'm a receptionist for an ophthalmologist." I'm a Cowboys fan, a father, a mother, a golfer, an accountant, I'm Irish, I'm Korean, I'm African American, I'm a Republican, a Democrat, an Independent, a Baptist, a Presbyterian, an agnostic, a spiritual seeker.

But who am I . . . really?

It's a confusing question in a time as fluid and fleeting as ours. When identities are as thin as Facebook profiles and as impermanent as the Instagram society flowing rapidly around us, we stammer at the question. In Judith Guest's novel *Ordinary People*, Calvin Jarrett is a husband and father whose older son has tragically died in a boating accident. The trauma of this loss pushes Calvin into a personal crisis, one in which he is plagued by the question, "Who in the hell are you?" The question is like a bad song stuck in his head, repeated over and over. He wonders, "Who can step in time to that music for more than thirty seconds?"[6]

Whenever Calvin is at a party, or in a bar, or passing by people on the street engaged in ordinary conversation, and he overhears the phrase, "Now, I'm the kind of man who . . ." he listens carefully, hoping for some clue to his own identity. But what he overhears never helps, and finally he comes to the sad conclusion, "I'm the kind of man who—hasn't the least idea what kind of man I am."[7]

The apostle Paul discovered that human beings cannot really respond to the question of identity simply by looking within. Identity, Paul believed, is a matter of looking outside ourselves to what genuinely matters in life and offering ourselves to that, which for Paul was the Christ who calls us as his own. Our identity rests ultimately not in the list of what we have achieved or acquired but in the One to whom we pour out our lives as an offering. Our life is hidden with Christ, and even so our death (Col. 3:3).

"Christ will be exalted now as always in my body," Paul, himself imprisoned, writes to the Philippians, "whether by life or by death" (1:20b).

"Who am I?" asked Bonhoeffer again at the end of his poem, still tormented by his solitary and anxious quest. But then he concluded, "Whoever I am, Thou knowest, O God, I am thine."[8]

Prayer for the Day

We are restless, O God, until we rest in Thee. We give thanks that you know who we are, that you claim us as your own, and that you bring our living and our dying to completion. Amen.

Last Will and Testament

Malachi 3:13–18

They shall be mine, says the LORD of hosts, my
special possession.
                                                    —Malachi 3:17a

At seventy-eight years old, Mary McLeod Bethune sat
at her desk in Daytona and penned her "Last Will and
Testament." After decades of working as a teacher and
public servant, founding a school for girls that became
a celebrated Historically Black College, serving on the
Roosevelt Administration, and managing a full calendar
of speaking engagements, one would think she had a great
deal to bequeath. She did not. "Truly my worldly posses-
sions are few. Yet, my experiences have been rich. From
them, I have distilled principles and policies in which
I believe firmly, for they represent the meaning of my
life's work."[9] Bethune proceeded to bequeath virtues to
the African American community. These included love,
hope, a thirst for education, respect for the use of power,
and faith. "Without faith, nothing is possible. With it,

nothing is impossible. Faith in God is the greatest power, but great, too is faith in oneself."[10]

Bethune was conscious of an alternate economy—a divine one in which virtue has immense value. She understood that some things are too precious to be monetized and that justice-seekers needed to be familiar with other metrics of valuation. While the struggle for justice demands changed outcomes, it would be naive to focus on outcomes alone. The imbalances of power in this world are too extreme for that—too likely to prompt despair on the inevitable occasions when the wicked will prosper and righteousness will seem pointless. In such moments we may be tempted to throw up our hands and say, "It is vain to serve God." Or we might ask, "What do we gain by keeping God's commands?" (Mal. 3:14).

But Bethune urges us not to despair. Our lives are not defined by acquisition, she seems to say, but by our union with God. This conviction, when ground deep in the soul, enlightens sages, emboldens revolutionaries, and gives certain elderly churchwomen a beeline to Jesus. So, in responding to the urgent cries for basic human necessities, it helps to remember that we are enveloped by another reality in which there is no meter for prestige or money or good looks or any power other than God's. This means accepting that there will always be a mismatch between God's vision of profit and the Dow Jones. And that differential is much like the contrast between worldly wisdom and God's foolishness, between earthly power and the weakness which is strength (1 Cor. 1:18–19; 2 Cor. 12:9). Buoyed by a power that exceeds our own, we can live lives worth emulating and leave legacies of love, hope, and endurance.

Prayer for the Day

Bear us up, gracious God, as we trust in your divine economy. Strengthen our resolve when evil seems to prevail. Teach us to treasure what you treasure and know that we are always held in your embrace. Amen.

Friends of the Kingdom

Luke 9:1–6

He sent them out to proclaim the kingdom of
God and to heal.

—Luke 9:2

U.S. soldiers on patrol carry as much as a hundred
pounds of equipment. When they are out on a mission,
they take such things as sleeping bags, canteens, food,
sunscreens, fire kits, medicine, sunglasses, GPS units,
cellular phones, knives, bayonets, handguns, rifles, gre-
nades, and extra clothing.

When Jesus sent his disciples out on the mission of
God's kingdom, he sent them with . . . nothing. "'Take
nothing for your journey,'" he told them, "no staff, nor
bag, nor bread, nor money—not even an extra tunic'"
(Luke 9:3). The mission of the military requires that
soldiers of war have all they need to defend themselves
against the enemy. Soldiers of the cross, by contrast, are
to be dependent upon those to whom they go. The ministry of Jesus looks not for enemies, but for friends, friends
of the kingdom. "Whatever house you enter," Jesus told

them on the way out the door, "stay there, and leave from there" (Luke 9:4).

It's not that there would not be enemies out there as well as friends. Jesus knew that. Whenever you meet lack of welcome, inhospitality, rejection, the back of the fist instead of the open hand, Jesus told them, then don't force the issue, simply move on. "As you are leaving that town," he said, "shake the dust off your feet" (Luke 9:5). But also look, said Jesus, for those who will receive you, welcome you, support you.

"Take Christ to the World," sings the mission hymn, but here is the irony of Christian mission: as we take Christ to the world, we find that Christ is already out there waiting for us, already present in the places where we go to serve.

In a seminary where I once taught, a student had been assigned to a large and affluent suburban church as a ministry intern, and he was discouraged. The church seemed to him to be rich and complacent, indifferent to the needs of society, and more concerned about matters like the décor of the bride's parlor than the plight of the poor in the city. Hearing the student complain loudly about his situation, a mentor at the seminary gave him some wise counsel. "Go back to this congregation," he advised, "and look for friends of the kingdom."

So he did, and gradually he found them, Christians in that church who were concerned about the needy, ready to serve as people of compassion and as healers for a broken world.

Not long ago, I spoke with a man whose wife died suddenly and unexpectedly of a heart attack. "The first few days were the roughest," he told me. "Everything in our home spoke her name and reminded me that she was gone."

The day after his wife died, the man's doorbell rang. It was a neighbor, a man whom he barely knew, standing on the step and holding a paper bag. "I am so sorry to hear about the loss of your wife," the neighbor said. Pointing to the bag, he added, "I have some hot soup, two bowls, and some spoons. May I split this with you?" The two of them sat at the table, and shared chicken soup and comfort in the midst of grief.

Because Christ is alive and at work in the world, they are out there—down the street, in every neighborhood and church, in every place far and near—friends of the kingdom, everywhere.

Prayer for the Day

Open our eyes, O Christ, to all those around us who love you and who serve your kingdom. When we see their mercy and compassion, allow our hope and faith to increase, through Christ our Lord. Amen.

Second Week of Advent

Day 1

Dawn from On High

Luke 1:68–79

"Blessed be the Lord God of Israel,
  for he has looked favorably on his people and
  redeemed them."
                                        —Luke 1:68

Several Black communities sprung up along the border between Canada and the U.S. prior to the Civil War. They had names like Africville, Bunnell's Landing, and Wilberforce Colony. One of them was called "Dawn."[1] For a time, Dawn had over 150 households, a large plot of communal farmland, and there were plans to build a manufacturing school.

The town's name seemed fitting for those who arrived after weeks of walking under the cover of darkness, perhaps led only by the North Star and the generosity of strangers. And the town's name seemed right for a community of people seeking to start over—people who suddenly had new names, identities, postures, gaits, responsibilities, and whole new lives to create. Even if they were fifty, sixty, or seventy years old, they were like newborns because much was still nascent in them. The fact that God had brought them to Canada—"the last gate before you got all the way *inside* of heaven"—served as a sign that God could be trusted with the future.[2] Their wounds and unanswered questions did not evaporate overnight. Like us, they had to raise their petitions to the Almighty and watch the answers unfold in the drama of life.

But maybe some mornings, Dawn's residents looked up into the blushing sky and thought not only about the surprising newness God ushers into our individual lives, but of the cosmic Dawn that is to come. Zechariah sings of its inbreaking:

> "By the tender mercy of our God,
>   the dawn from on high will break upon us,
> to give light to those who sit in darkness and in the
>   shadow of death,
> to guide our feet into the way of peace."
> (Luke 1:78–79)

More beautiful than we can imagine, this ethereal dawn marks the advent of endless peace. Death's grip will loosen. The violence and alienation that stalk us will cease. The memories that shake us will lose their power and an altogether different mode of relating will begin. When? We can't know. But we can practice enacting this peace each day. Oh, we will stumble again and again—we cannot perfect it. But we have the model of Jesus, who guides our feet in the path of peace. And the God of all tenderness gives us holy leadings and reminders to be patient with all that is unresolved within us.

I am convinced that every morning God paints a wordless oracle in the sky. Sometimes it is a burst of coral. Sometimes there are ribbons of lavender. Sometimes there is a vanishing whirl of pink and gold—gone before we can even discern its subtle shades. Each time, something glorious happens in the pastel haze: God gives us a sign of the coming Dawn and blesses all that is still nascent in our lives.

Prayer for the Day

Alpha and Omega, thank you for the gift of another day. Only you know what the hours before us hold and what will be required of us, but you promise us your presence, your strength, your peace. Bless us as this new day unfolds. Amen.

The Invisibility of Hope

Romans 8:22–25

> Now hope that is seen is not hope. For who hopes for what is seen? But if we hope for what we do not see, we wait for it with patience.
> —Romans 8:24b–25

Years ago, when Lesley Stahl was the CBS News White House correspondent, there was a late-breaking story involving President Reagan. Lesley scrambled to cover it in time for the broadcast that night, and she managed to file the story barely before deadline. She did not, however, have time to get a film crew to the White House, so, to accompany her report, she borrowed stock video footage from the White House Office of Communications.

That evening, Stahl gave her report about what had happened at the White House, while on the screen flashed brightly lit pictures of the president standing in front of waving American flags and riding horses through the surf on a California beach. The next day, the head of White House communications called Stahl to congratulate her on her report. She expressed thanks for the word of encouragement but added that maybe words of thanks were out of place because, after all, her report had been sharply critical of the president.

"Oh yeah," said the White House official. "Your words were critical, but you showed my pictures. In the battle between the eye and the ear, the eye wins every time."[3]

The Christian faith is, in a deep sense, a wager on the truth of the very opposite, that in the battle between what we *see* around us and the promises of the gospel we *hear*, what we hear ultimately prevails. That's what Paul means when he writes to the Romans, "For in hope we were saved. Now hope that is seen is not hope. For who hopes for what is seen? But if we hope for what we do not see, we wait for it with patience" (Rom. 8:24–25).

What we see, of course, is the regular round of discouragement that saturates the news on television every day—the grinding accounts of crime and violence, the economic struggles faced by so many, the health threats, the declining environment. Sometimes there is even a warning, "Viewer Discretion Advised," meaning that if you watch this story you will see potentially disturbing events that expose you to the raw reality of life in our time.

Paul knows the hard truths of our world. As for the turmoil we see around us, Paul says it is the creation "groaning in labor pains." What we can see is troubling, the many sufferings of our unsettled time; what we hope for is what we cannot yet see but which God promises, "that the creation itself will be set free from its bondage to decay and will obtain the freedom of the glory of the children of God" (Rom. 8:21–22).

When we squint and look more closely at our world, we can see even now shoots of green in the desert, rays of light shining even now in the darkness. Here are people feeding the hungry, there are compassionate caregivers caring for the dying in hospices, over there are people advocating for a more just society, and here are teachers serving tirelessly in struggling schools. For those who trust the good news of the gospel, these are places in our present world where we can place our wagers—set down our stack of chips, so to speak—saying through our labors and our prayers, "I am wagering that God's future belongs to such as these, and I am waiting in patience for the coming glory of God's children."

Prayer for the Day

We confess, O God, that we are often dismayed by the world we see around us. Wrong seems to be in charge, evil rules the fevered nations, and suffering is the everyday cup of bitterness for so many. Give us a hope for what we cannot yet fully see, the coming of your redemption in Jesus Christ, in whose name we pray. Amen.

All We Need

2 Peter 1:2–15

His divine power has given us everything needed
for life and godliness, through the knowledge of
him who called us by his own glory and goodness.
—2 Peter 1:3

My grandfather, George, was raised by his grandmother,
Martha, who became blind in her later years. As a young
boy, my grandfather used to lead her around the small
Georgia town where they lived. He would lead her to the
bank to pay bills, to the store to buy groceries, and to
the pharmacy for medicine. Yet, it was always clear that
she, being a rather strong-willed personality, was doing
the directing. The two of them became a memorable pair
around town, and they developed a deep bond. He always
remembered the words she spoke to him on her deathbed.
"George, I've led you as far as I can lead you." There was
no irony in this line for him because she had truly been
his guide and his caregiver. Blindness had not hindered
her mothering. But it took a while for my grandfather to
recognize the great well of strength and resilience that

she had fostered in him. She had prepared him to move through the world without her guidance.

The author of Second Peter tries to mother the Christian family in a similar way. The letter is a farewell address that assures the Christian community of God's power and promises. Soon they would no longer have their guiding patriarch, but in God, they would find everything they would ever need. They had not been left to their own resources. In fact, they had absorbed lessons from church leaders and were already faithful discerners of the Spirit's leading. They had inner wisdom but just did not realize it.

When it comes to spirituality, we don't often realize that what we have in God is enough. Surely American consumerism contributes to this feeling. Contemporary visions of spiritual thriving tend to be a little too romantic or heroic, leading us to believe that our human efforts determine God's action in our souls. But we are the receivers in the divine-human encounter. Grace pours into our feeble hands—whether open or closed. In God, we have all we need.

Perhaps Evelyn Underhill says it best when she explains that authentic prayer

> places our souls at the disposal of the immanent Spirit. In other words, it promotes abandonment to God; and this in order that the soul's separate activity may more and more be invaded, transfigured, and at last superseded by the unmeasured Divine action. In Pauline language, maturity of soul is to be gauged by the extent in which the Spirit "prays in us."[4]

And, if the Spirit is praying in us, if we are channels for God's radiance, then there is no need for gimmicks or charlatans who purport to have more spiritual power than we do. Indeed, God has quite a track record of putting our doubts and insecurities to good use.

The challenge, of course, is to follow the Spirit's mysterious leading, trusting that grace flows not only through the wise and suave outliers in the human family but through the quirky, the frail, the wavering, and the confused—through people like ourselves. God makes *us* mediators of sublime power. "His divine power has given us everything needed for life and godliness, through the knowledge of him who called us by his own glory and goodness" (2 Pet. 1:3).

Prayer for the Day

Loving God, you are all we need. Day by day, your soft hand guides us in the way of truth. Help us to rest in your love and power this day and always. Amen.

The Disappointing Jesus

Luke 7:18–30

> "Are you the one who is to come, or are we to
> wait for another?"
>   —Luke 7:19

John the Baptist had great expectations for Jesus. "I baptize you with water," he said, but the one I am expecting
"will baptize you with the Holy Spirit and fire." Not only
will this expected one offer a potent baptism, he will also
drain the religious swamp of those who are unworthy.
"His winnowing fork is in his hand," trumpeted John, "to
clear his threshing floor . . . the chaff he will burn with
unquenchable fire" (Luke 3:16–17).

John was soon locked up when his preaching turned
to prophetic meddling in King Herod's personal life
(Luke 3:19–20). Being jailed by the king is not pleasant,
of course, but John was probably not shaken to his roots.
He was surely convinced that his work would go on in
an even more powerful way. Jesus, the hoped-for Mes-
siah, was already active in the world, and John no doubt

expected to be able to see from his cell the smoke rising from the fires of zeal and reform that Jesus would ignite.

But then the reports started coming in: Jesus was not swinging a scythe but doing ministry with a gentle word and a healing touch. He cleansed a leper, healed a paralytic, restored a man with a withered hand, and even cured the slave of a Gentile army officer. This was not what John expected. It was not revolutionary enough, and, dismayed, John sent two disciples to ask Jesus, "Are you the one who is to come, or are we to wait for another?" (Luke 7:19).

John was not the only person to be disappointed in Jesus. He was simply one of the first. When Thomas Jefferson was president of the United States, he read the New Testament and was disappointed as well. The Jesus he found there was too complex, too cluttered by what Jefferson considered to be fables. The Jesus Jefferson wanted was a simple moralist who taught "pure deism." In short, he wanted a Jesus just like himself. So, as religion scholar Stephen Prothero says, "Jefferson sat down in the White House, razor in hand, and began to cut and paste his own Bible." When he did so, "the American Jesus was born."[5]

Most of us do not take a razor to the New Testament, but we do have a picture of Jesus tailored to our own vision, a Jesus we are hoping for and expecting. But by the grace of God, it is the real Jesus who comes, not the Jesus of our limited desires. The Jesus we await in Advent comes to us as our Savior, and, ironically, Jesus sometimes saves us by fulfilling our deepest hopes and other times by disappointing our narrow wishes. As a priest friend said to essayist Anne Lamott, "You can safely assume you've created God in your own image when it turns out that

God hates all the same people you do."[6] We do not get to create Jesus in our image; thankfully Jesus Christ comes to restore God's image in us. The Jesus who comes to us is wider in mercy, deeper in grace, more tender in compassion, more powerful in justice than our small imaginations could ever expect.

Maturity in faith is measured in part by our willingness to let our small expectations of Jesus be enlarged by the capacious truth of his presence. As Jesus replied to John's disciples, "'Go and tell John what you have seen and heard: the blind receive their sight, the lame walk, the lepers are cleansed, the deaf hear, the dead are raised, the poor have good news brought to them. And blessed is anyone who takes no offense at me'" (Luke 7:22–23).

Prayer for the Day

Come, thou long-expected Jesus. Come to us as you truly are, and not only as we wish you were. Come to us as God's own Son and our Savior, with healing in your wings. Amen.

When We Sing

Isaiah 12:2–6

Sing praises to the LORD, for he has done
> gloriously;
> let this be known in all the earth.
Shout aloud and sing for joy, O royal Zion,
> for great in your midst is the Holy One of
> Israel.

—Isaiah 12:5–6

Not long ago, I was doing some research and came across a recording of Henri Nouwen. I thought it contained a lecture but when I pressed Play, I was awed to hear him singing. There was something arresting about the purity of his voice. The song, "Ubi Caritas," seemed to come from the deepest part of his being—as if no one was there to hear the song but God. Only others *were* present. Before long, Henri was leading his audience in song. They sounded reluctant at first, but Henri kept coaching them, urging them to sing from the center of themselves. Even on the recording I could sense the energy shifting in the room as they sang. As their attention fastened on

God, the sound became heavy and spacious and consuming. If Henri hadn't intervened to curb the song, I suspect the group could have sung for an hour or more.

Song is the soul's mother tongue and favored mode of expression. Somehow our convictions and longings surface and deep truths that hover at the edge of consciousness seep out. Usually only the simplest words are nimble enough to initiate this flow. The French mystic Madeleine Delbrêl suggests that a spiritual unlocking takes place; music enchants us out of ourselves and enlivens us in the process.[7] Whatever the mysterious workings, what is clear is that we are creatures of adoration. Song serves as a crucial way of knowing God and ourselves and a conduit for divine energy. Hidden dimensions of God's joy become available to us when we sing, and the Lord's presence feels more palpable.

When we've lost our way or feel pummeled by despair, the Spirit soothes us or even emboldens us through song. This happened so often for Bernice Johnson Reagon during the civil rights era that she described the protests in Albany, Georgia, as a "singing movement."[8] Singing "This May Be the Last Time" steeled protestors before demonstrations and singing "We Shall Overcome" and "This Little Light of Mine" stirred them during marches and in the aftermath as they sat in hot jail cells. A fitting song would rise in one person's heart and soon the whole group would be borne up by its power.

Hildegard of Bingen goes so far as to say we never stop singing. She says our beating hearts and rhythmic breath form part of the musical score of creation. We raise a song with chirping birds and crashing waves and with stars that bellow like tubas in the dark.[9] The universe rings with God's praise. "Shout aloud and sing for joy,

O royal Zion, for great in your midst is the Holy One of Israel" (Isa. 12:6).

Prayer for the Day

Loving God, you are the source of all music. Your goodness reaches beyond language and logic to the core of our being. Let a song of praise arise in us. May its melody of hope be discerned by all we meet. Amen.

Day 6

Generosity

2 Corinthians 9:1–15

He who supplies seed to the sower and bread for
food will supply and multiply your seed for sow-
ing and increase the harvest of your righteousness.
—2 Corinthians 9:10

A young mother I know has figured out a way to handle
a recurring problem with her two daughters. Sometimes
when she is pushing her grocery cart through the checkout
lane, she will relent to her children's request for a candy
bar. But she buys only one and divides it evenly between
the two children. The problem was that she could never
get the division exactly right. Inevitably one child would
protest loudly, "No fair! Her part is bigger!" So, this mom
fell upon an elegant solution: let one daughter divide the
candy bar in half and then let the other daughter choose
which of the two halves she wants. Fair is fair.

In many areas of life, fairness is a good thing. We want
fair wages, fair housing, and fair practices in our courts.
We make an ethical case for serving fair trade coffee in

our church fellowship halls. Fairness rests on impartiality and even-handedness. Fairness seeks to ensure that every person and group gets what they genuinely deserve. One of the first disputes among early Christians involved the charge of "No fair!" by the Hellenists, Greek-speaking Christians, complaining that their widows were receiving less from the charitable food pantry than were the widows of the Hebrews, Aramaic-speakers (see Acts 6:1). Fair is fair.

The gospel, however, ultimately troubles all of our notions of fairness. The God of Jesus Christ is not fair. The God of Jesus Christ is generous. The God of Jesus Christ is not impartial and even-handed. The God of Jesus Christ takes our side and is our advocate, the God who gives us every day far more than we could ask or deserve. "Do not forget all his benefits," sings the psalmist, "who forgives all your iniquity, who heals all your diseases, who redeems your life from the Pit, who crowns you with steadfast love and mercy" (Ps. 103:2–4).

The mother who wisely practices strict fairness in dividing candy bars acts differently in the weightier areas of life. If one of her daughters has a fever, she does not dispassionately say, "Well, I gave your sister a half hour of my time this afternoon, and that's what you will get, too. Fair is fair." No, she stays up with her child through the night, wiping her brow and speaking soothingly. If her other daughter has a bad day at school, she holds her tightly in love for as long as she needs. She may seek fairness with candy bars, but she shows generosity with her love.

"God is able to provide you with every blessing in abundance, so that by always having enough of everything, you may share abundantly in every good work," writes Paul

(2 Cor. 9:8). In other words, it is gratitude for the generosity of God that leads us to live a life of generosity.

There are practical implications. Consider, for example, the thorny matter of immigration. We cannot make immigration policy out of the New Testament, of course, but we can think about immigration in the light of God's generosity. It does not go far enough simply to say, "If you break the law, then you face the consequences. Fair is fair." As one evangelical Christian group that studied the issues discovered, the gospel calls us not to cold legalism but to generosity, and "the motivations behind this generous spirit were that the people of God were not to forget that they had been strangers in Egypt . . . and that God loved the foreigner."[10] Because of God's own generosity to us, we can be abundant in generosity to others.

Prayer for the Day

O God, you have given us every good gift of mercy, compassion, and grace. Let us open our hands and our hearts in gratitude by seeking to be as generous to others as you have been to us in Jesus Christ, in whose name we pray. Amen.

Day 7

God Sees the Effort

Amos 9:8–15

On that day I will raise up
  the booth of David that is fallen,
and repair its breaches,
  and raise up its ruins,
  and rebuild it as in the days of old.
                    —Amos 9:11

Anyone who has worked for an extended period behind the scenes, anyone who has done the daily work of caring for another person, who has cooked thankless meals and then loaded the dishwasher so the other person could rest, or helped someone bathe and dress, or changed their diaper, or balanced their pills in one hand and their glass of juice in another, or sat in traffic listening to their favorite music while driving them to the doctor or the dentist or the pharmacy or the physical therapist, and then lain awake at night and worried about how to pay the bills, occasionally needs a reminder that God sees the effort.

No labor is invisible to God. Not the labor done in slippers or bathrobes, nor the quiet labor done outside of our homes—arriving early to make the coffee for the AA meeting, staying late to clean up after the church dinner and walk bags of trash to the dumpster. None of this labor is invisible to God. And God knows how wearying it is and what it costs us to do it.

The 2009 film *Philosopher Kings* explores the lives of janitors at several large American universities. Viewers get a window into the daily challenge of clearing clogged toilets, arranging chairs, mopping floors, and emptying trash. Viewers also get a sense of what it means to do this work in plain sight and yet be ignored or in some cases shunned. Evil social hierarchies prevent students, faculty, and other staff members from seeing how wonderful the custodians are. Oscar loves to fish. Jim plays in a band that once opened for the Beach Boys. Corby is an artist who drives a van styled like Scooby Doo's "Mystery Machine." Josue designs a water delivery system for a rural community in Haiti. Whether we realize it or not, there is a loss that comes when we fail to see one another.

Sometimes we develop this awareness in hindsight. Robert Hayden remembers his father's tireless labors in a poem, "Those Winter Sundays." Hayden's father had a morning ritual of rising early to make a fire and shine his son's shoes, but at the time the boy sees none of this. Only later does he appreciate the affection in his father's efforts and recognize "love's austere and lonely offices."[11]

But there is no progressive realization for God. God sees the labor in the moment. We are never out of God's sight or beyond God's reach. As Julian of Norwich says, "He is our clothing, wrapping and enveloping us for love, embracing us and guiding us in all things, hanging about us in tender love, so that he can never leave us."[12]

And because God knows that thankless effort for the benefit of others can produce a sense of scarcity, God promises restoration and abundance. "I will restore the fortunes of my people Israel" (Amos 9:14a). God promises that those who plant vineyards will sit and enjoy the wine, that those who tend gardens will relax and feast on their fruits. Labor done for the benefit of others will be rewarded and respite will come. We can trust God's promise because God also has a long history of working in the background. And we can trust the Spirit to bear us up as we work for a just society in which all labor is honored.

Prayer for the Day

God of the Shadows, you are always working quietly behind the scenes—healing, comforting, nurturing growth. When our efforts go unnoticed and our labors are ignored, assure us that we are always in your sight. Help us to remember that your greatest miracle took place in a darkened tomb. Amen.

Third Week of Advent

God the Gardener

Luke 3:7–18

"I baptize you with water; but one who is more powerful than I is coming."

—Luke 3:16

A couple of years back, a thoughtful friend gave my wife and me a lovely, single-stem orchid plant with a beautiful white bloom. We carefully read the accompanying card that gave instructions for care. "It needs good light, but cannot withstand direct sunlight," were among the warnings, so we placed the plant on a table near, but not under, a window.

Three weeks later, disaster. The bloom was gone, the few leaves that hadn't dropped off were crinkled and brown, and the stem was clearly drooping. The poor orchid had fallen victim to a simple misunderstanding. I thought my wife was taking charge of the watering, and she thought I was.

"We'll know better next time," I said. "I'll toss it."

According to the Gospel of Luke, John the Baptist had something of the same instincts for gardening that

I do. Out on the banks of the Jordan River, John faced a sere and stiff-necked crowd and gave them a stark greeting: "You brood of vipers! Who warned you to flee from the wrath to come?" (Luke 3:7). Seeing no evidence of fruitfulness in their lives, he declared that he was ready to toss them out altogether. "Even now," he thundered, "the ax is lying at the root of the trees; every tree therefore that does not bear fruit is cut down and thrown into the fire" (Luke 3:9).

As I reached for the desiccated orchid to take it to the trash can, my wife gently touched my arm. "Let me try something," she said. She brought a glass of water from the kitchen and slowly drizzled water at the base of the plant, gently stirring the caked soil as she poured. Every day thereafter, she did the same, until one day, the plant miraculously sprung back to life. Two years later, it still bears white blooms, rescued by my wife's patience.

Later in Luke, we learn the good news that God is a gardener, too, and that, fortunately, God's gardening is more like my wife's than mine. Jesus tells the story of a man who had a fig tree that wasn't bearing fruit. The man, disgusted that the barren tree was wasting soil, ordered it cut down, but the man's gardener said, "Let's give it some more time. I'd like to try something" (see Luke 13:6–9).

In those places in life where things seem hopeless, it is God's patient way to "give it more time." A by-product of our frazzled and contentious society is the pressure to lose patience, which, in many ways, is the same as losing hope. A person makes a mistake in public, and social media fills up with demands that this person be rebuked, scorned, fired, banished. How quickly we lose patience with our neighbors, our families, perhaps even ourselves. "Let's toss it," we say. "Even now," we threaten, "the ax is poised to swing."

But it is deep good news that God is not this kind of gardener. God's love is patient, and, as the psalmist sings, "the steadfast love of the LORD is from everlasting to everlasting" (Ps. 103:17). I am especially grateful for this when I remember those seasons in my own life when the blooms had dropped away, the leaves had turned brown, and my spirit drooped. It was then that I felt the tender care of God, pouring the water of life around me, gently stirring the soil, mercifully nurturing me back to life.

Prayer for the Day

Teach us patience, O merciful God. Let us be as gentle, nurturing, and life-giving to others as you always are to us in Jesus Christ, in whose name we pray. Amen.

Day 2

"As the Waters Cover the Sea"

Isaiah 11:1–9

> They will not hurt or destroy
> on all my holy mountain;
> for the earth will be full of the knowledge of the
> LORD
> as the waters cover the sea.
>
> —Isaiah 11:9

The Rocks of Saint Peter and Saint Paul lie about 700 miles off the coast of Brazil in the center of the Atlantic Ocean. Their rough terrain and sparse vegetation draw few visitors other than sea fowl, but they have a hidden splendor. These little islands are mountain summits in one of the world's longest mountain ranges: the Atlantic Ridge.

Under water, the mountains carve a majestic "S" in the center of the ocean. Shrouded in silt, they stand like a family in procession 10,000 miles long. With the right camera, one can see the resemblance in their bare, rocky slopes.[1] But, huddled as they are in the dark deep, their crevices and folds are only visible to sea life and oceanographers.

Now it is unlikely that Isaiah had undersea mountains in mind when he gave his oracle about God's peace, but they shed light on the meaning of his prophecy. "They will not hurt or destroy on all my holy mountain, for the earth will be full of the knowledge of the LORD as the waters cover the sea." The Atlantic Ridge gives us a sense of how much water covers the sea—enough to hide a 10,000-mile mountain range! God's peace will engulf the world conflicts that dominate the landscape of history. All of the confusion, all of the worries, all of the painful memories, and every one of the doubts that plague us will be subsumed in an ocean of peace.

Clearly, the peace God promises is from another realm, but we can participate in it now. We can follow God's current of grace and float odd virtues like gentleness and meekness that rarely seem to have a place on shore. We can shed the crusty defenses we have built up "for the earth will be full of the knowledge of God as the waters cover the sea."

Carried by the sea's mysterious rhythm, maybe we will finally discover our true oneness with God's creation. Rachel Carson revels in this unity. "Fish, amphibian, and reptile, warm-blooded bird and mammal—each of us carries in our veins a salty stream in which the elements sodium, potassium, and calcium are combined in almost the same proportions as in sea water."[2] If we have biochemical similarities, doesn't this suggest that we have the potential to live in harmony? Doesn't this suggest that, as Isaiah says, peace is our destiny?

When justice and peace feel elusive, when the enemies of peace rage with unprecedented power, it helps to follow the model of the undersea mountains. Calmly, they urge us not to grow weary or shrink back, but to be strong and steady—bold witnesses to the coming peace of God.

Prayer for the Day

God of all serenity, your peace knows no bounds and your vision for wholeness always exceeds human imagination. Prepare us for the gentle world that is to come. Help us now to be vessels of your grace driven by the invisible current of the Spirit. We pray in the holy name of Jesus. Amen.

The Peaceful Kingdom

Isaiah 11:1–9

The wolf shall live with the lamb,
   the leopard shall lie down with the kid,
the calf and the lion and the fatling together,
   and a little child shall lead them.
                                        —Isaiah 11:6

People of faith have always dreamed of a time when God will bring perfect peace. John in the book of Revelation dreamed that God "will wipe every tear from their eyes. Death will be no more; mourning and crying and pain will be no more" (Rev. 21:4). Jeremiah hoped for a great day when God's law would be written in people's hearts, and no teachers would be needed because "they shall all know me, from the least of them to the greatest" (Jer. 31:34). The prophet Isaiah spoke of the dream using a beautiful image of *shalom*, of all nature at peace: "the wolf shall live with the lamb, the leopard shall lie down with the kid" (Isa. 11:6).

For some people, all of these dreams of God's peace are just that—dreams. They are, some say, too idealistic, too "pie in the sky," too out of touch with the rough-and-tumble realities of life. "The lion will lie down with the lamb," Woody Allen famously quipped, "but the lamb won't get much sleep." One contemporary hymn speaks of a faith rooted in the here and now and scorns the pie-in-the-sky hope of "some heaven light years away."[3]

But the biblical visions of God's peaceful kingdom are not merely sweet and pious otherworldly sentiments. They are, to the contrary, affirmations of trust in God's goodness and sources of courage and hope precisely in the midst of life's struggles. It is an irony of faith that the promises of God always look perilously fragile, always appear to be no match for real life. Biblical scholars remind us that Isaiah's vision of God's *shalom* came when Jerusalem was at one of its weakest points, when God's people were at the mercy of powerful enemies. And who could have imagined that the promised Christ child, whom we await in this season of Advent, born a vulnerable infant amid the tyranny of Rome, would one day stand in Easter glory because not even a Roman cross could defeat him?

The Christian life is a wager that the promises of God and the hope for God's peaceful kingdom are finally truer than the jackboot, the tyrant, and all of the cruelties of history. That's why Martin Luther in "A Mighty Fortress" could sing, "And though this world, with devils filled, should threaten to undo us, we will not fear, for God has willed his truth to triumph through us. . . . The body they may kill: God's truth abideth still; his kingdom is forever!"

In the early 1990s, author and activist Jonathan Kozol spent time doing research in the South Bronx, which was then among the poorest and most violent areas in the country. He met a remarkable thirteen-year-old boy named Anthony, a deeply spiritual young man who told Kozol about his own dream of God's kingdom:

> God will be there. . . . All friendly animals will be there, but no mean ones. As for television, forget it! If you want vision, you can use your eyes to see the people that you love. All the people from the street will be there. My uncle will be there and he will be healed. You won't see him buying drugs. . . . No violence will there be in heaven. . . . You'll recognize all the children who have died when they were little. Jesus will be good to them and play with them. At night he'll come and visit at your house. God will be fond of you.[4]

The streets of the South Bronx remained drug-ridden and violent despite Anthony's dream. But his confidence in God's kingdom gave him the eyes of compassion for others and the ability to live in the grim environment with hope that the love of Jesus for children abides eternally. As Anthony knew in his heart, violence will one day pass away, but the kindness of God is forever.

Prayer for the Day

O God, your promise of peace came to us as a little child, a vulnerable infant born into an often cruel and violent world. Give to us a deeper trust in Christ, and a greater confidence in your promises, that we may live each day in hope. Amen.

Spiritual Maturity

Luke 7:31–35

"Wisdom is vindicated by all her children."
—Luke 7:35

What are the signs of spiritual maturity? With all our various devotional practices, how do we know if we are in fact growing in our faith and not simply spinning our wheels? After all, spiritual maturity cannot be measured in the typical ways we measure growth or expertise, and the particulars of our life circumstances make comparisons difficult, if not impossible.

Over the centuries, mystics and great spiritual teachers have offered libraries full of wisdom on these questions. For instance, Saint John Climacus, a seventh-century monk, wrote *The Ladder of Divine Ascent*.[5] John's ladder had thirty rather cryptic rungs to holiness beginning with renunciation of the world. For him, spiritual maturity was largely a matter of yielding certain vices like #11, talking too much; #12, lying; and #16, avarice, while developing a set of essential virtues like #24, simplicity, and #25, humility. Instead of a ladder, Western Christian spirituality has offered the trio of purgation, illumination, and union. For the most part, these follow a cyclical pattern and spiritual growth takes the form of a long and continuous spiral.

Jesus takes a more holistic approach in affirming the biblical command to "'love the Lord your God with all your heart, and with all your soul, and with all your strength, and with all your mind; and your neighbor as yourself'" (Luke 10:27). Loving God and neighbor naturally results in virtues like simplicity and humility without the need for scales or benchmarks.

Jesus does, however, point to signs of spiritual immaturity. Among these is the tendency of insisting on our own way.

> "To what then will I compare the people of this generation, and what are they like? They are like children sitting in the marketplace and calling to one another,
>
> 'We played the flute for you, and you did not dance; we wailed, and you did not weep.'"
>
> (Luke 7:31–32)

Here, Jesus names the problem of devising a script for God to follow and playing puppeteer. In these instances, we become like adorable-but-cranky children—resisting every toy presented to us as well as joy itself.

Thankfully, another spiritual teacher developed an antidote for this problem, too. Saint Ignatius of Loyola gave us the examen prayer as a tool to draw nearer to God through self-examination. The prescription is to turn our attention to God, give thanks for the blessings of the day, and then play the day back like a video. Where were the high moments and where were the low ones? Did we refuse gestures of love at any point? Did we resist God's joy? Why? These questions make it easier to have a real conversation with God and experience a flood of grace. We come to know that even if we are a mess, we are God's mess. And usually, an attention shift takes place. The spotlight turns from us to God, the source of all wisdom, love, and possibility, the one in whom "we live and move and have our being" (Acts 17:28).

> When we see no startling marks of our own religious progress or our usefulness to God, it is well to remember the babe in the stable and the little boy in the streets of Nazareth. The very life was there present, which was to change the whole history of the human race, the rescuing action of God. At that stage there was not much to show for it; yet there is perfect continuity between the stable and the Easter garden, and the thread that unites them is the hidden will of God.[6]

Prayer for the Day

Wise and loving God, you are still molding us, still leading us to spiritual maturity. Bring to our awareness, as only you know how, the ways we need to grow. Give us that holy wisdom that is born of prayerful reflection. Day by day, may we grow more dependent on your grace, more open to your leading, more conscious of your love. Amen.

Sisyphus and Jesus

Hebrews 10:10–18

"I will remember their sins and their lawless deeds no more."
—Hebrews 10:17

In Greek mythology, Sisyphus, the king of Corinth, was known as a crafty trickster, even able at times to pull a fast one on the gods. In the *Iliad*, Homer calls him "the most cunning of all men." But, as the myth goes, when Sisyphus died, Zeus himself designed a terrible punishment for this cunning deceiver. For all of eternity, Sisyphus would be condemned to roll a heavy rock up a long and steep hill in Hades. But every time Sisyphus would get the rock nearly to the top of the hill, it would slip from his grasp and roll back to the valley below, and Sisyphus would have to go down and start all over again. An endless and finally pointless task.

Sometimes life itself can seem like the punishment of Sisyphus, a ceaseless round of the same old, same old. "Another day, another dollar," we say, meaning that tomorrow will come and we will head out the door to do this all over again. Even our faith can feel Sisyphean. Jesus calls us to love our neighbor as ourselves, and so we try. But tomorrow the neighbor is still there, Jesus is still calling us to love, and so little seems changed. The rock has rolled back to the bottom of the hill.

According to the book of Hebrews, even the priests in the ancient Temple must have felt that they had been given the punishment of Sisyphus. Every day, these old priests would stand at the altar, saying the prayers, and making the offerings for the sins of the people. But the sins continued, and so did the prayers and the sacrifices— day after day, the same old, same old.

When the novelist Annie Dillard lived for a while in solitude on the Puget Sound, she made her way on Sundays to a small church in the fir trees. The minister of the church "knows God," she says. One Sunday, Dillard reports, the minister did this:

> Once, in the middle of the long pastoral prayer of intercession for the whole world—for the gift of wisdom to its leaders, for hope and mercy to the grieving and pained, succor to the oppressed, and God's grace to all—in the middle of this he stopped, and burst out, "Lord, we bring you these same petitions every week." After a shocked pause, he continued reading the prayer. Because of this, I like him very much.[7]

The minister was voicing both his faith—crying out boldly to God—and his frustration. "We bring you these same prayers every week," he cried out. Like Sisyphus of old, the pastor felt as though he was pushing the same rock up the hill over and over again.

But Hebrews wants us to know the refreshing good news of the gospel. Jesus is not like Zeus; we are not like Sisyphus. Jesus walked into the great heavenly sanctuary and made his offering for our sin—the offering of his very own sinless self—"once for all" (Heb. 10:10). And then "'he sat down at the right hand of God'" (Heb. 10:12). Jesus sat down because he is in charge, but he sat down also because the job was done, finished. The stone of human sin did not roll back down the hill but was rolled away forever, like the stone rolled away at the empty tomb.

Because Jesus acted "once and for all," we can view each day as fresh and new, full of faith and hope, and be ready anew to "provoke one another to love and good deeds" (Heb. 10:24).

Prayer for the Day

Come to us in our weariness, O God of hope, with your refreshing mercy. Enable us to greet each new day not as a time of ceaseless toil but as those who say, "This is the day you have made. Let us rejoice and be glad in it." In the name of the Christ who offered himself once and for all. Amen.

You Have Our Attention

Isaiah 42:10–18

Let the sea roar and all that fills it,
    the coastlands and their inhabitants.
Let the desert and its towns lift up their voice,
    the villages that Kedar inhabits;
let the inhabitants of Sela sing for joy,
    let them shout from the tops of the mountains.
                    —Isaiah 42:10b–11

When it comes to attention-grabbers in Scripture, the maternal images of God are in a class by themselves. They offer us surprising clues into who God is. Sometimes we get a sense of God's affection for us:

Yet it was I who taught Ephraim to walk,
    I took them up in my arms;
        but they did not know that I healed them.
I led them with cords of human kindness,
    with bands of love.
I was to them like those

who lift infants to their cheeks.
I bent down to them and fed them.

(Hos. 11:3–4)

On other occasions, we see God's concern for us in moments of distress: "As a mother comforts her child, so I will comfort you; you shall be comforted in Jerusalem" (Isa. 66:13). And God reminds us that even though we may feel insignificant or forgotten, we are always on God's mind, "Can a woman forget her nursing child, or show no compassion for the child of her womb? Even these may forget, yet I will not forget you. See, I have inscribed you on the palms of my hands" (Isa. 49:15–16).

But not all the images of Mama God are as sweet. We also see God's urgency. "For a long time I have held my peace, I have kept still and restrained myself; now I will cry out like a woman in labor, I will gasp and pant" (Isa. 42:14). This is not a sentimental moment. This is an encounter with a God who screams, grips our hands, and clutches our clothing to get our attention. The Almighty is shaking up the whole creation—leveling mountains, drying up pools, and moving in a whole new direction. We don't know where God is going, but she is taking us with her—dragging us if she must. God is giving birth to something new and guess what? *We* are her midwives!

Never been a midwife before? No problem. Our work is to watch and listen and stay in rhythm as best we can. We trust God's timing, not our own. It's all about remembering that we are in transition and things can intensify at any moment. Stay loose. Look for small shifts in energy. Singing sometimes helps, at least in the beginning. As things progress, expect a need for more silence—but no guarantees here. Every experience of labor is unique.

Oh—and there are a couple of "Don'ts." Don't tell God what to do or how to do it. That would be very, *very* bad.

Prayer for the Day

Screaming God, you have our attention. Help us to listen. Help us to improvise. Help us to trust that you are bearing gifts in your own time. Ready us for the change to come. Amen.

Day 7

The Bread of Tears

Psalm 80:1–7

Restore us, O God of hosts;
  let your face shine, that we may be saved.
                         —Psalm 80:7

In Psalm 80, the psalmist prays during a time of national trouble. Some unnamed threat has arisen, some crisis has occurred, and the people are in peril. "Stir up your might," the psalmist desperately pleads to heaven, "and come to save us!" (v. 2). Before crying out to God for help, the psalmist recalls better days. The psalmist remembers that in the past God had been a shepherd to Israel, the kind of loving guide who fed the people with goodness and filled their cups to overflowing. But now, in these days of trouble, he says that God "has fed them with the bread of tears" (v. 5).

The bread of tears—what a curious and compelling image. We think of God's table as a place of feasting and joy. "On this mountain," the prophet Isaiah promises, "the LORD of hosts will make for all peoples a feast of rich food, a feast of well-aged wines" (Isa. 25:6). But the

69

psalmist realizes that, in a troubled time, instead of succulent lamb, the wine of gladness, and milk and honey, the menu at God's table has changed to the bread of tears.

How can our tears feed us? Sometimes it is tearful anguish over trouble, grief over what we have lost, that summons us to a deeper faith and feeds our hope. On a rainy evening in March of 2020, Pope Francis stood in the gloom of an empty St. Peter's Square and spoke to a world driven to fear and grief by a worldwide pandemic. "Thick darkness has gathered over our squares, our streets and our cities," he said. "It has taken over our lives, filling everything with a deafening silence and a distressing void."[8] But then, the pope acknowledged that the crisis, as severe as it was, had interrupted the lives of a world that had come to think it was self-sufficient, a world that had been on a seemingly unblocked course of narcissism and greed. "Faith begins," said the pope, "when we realize we are in need of salvation. We are not self-sufficient; by ourselves we flounder: we need the Lord, like ancient navigators needed the stars."[9] Like the psalmist before him, Francis recognized that the world's tears were actually feeding a return to faith. "Lord, you are calling to us," he prayed, "calling us to faith."[10]

Philosopher George Yancy, who is an atheist, recently interviewed Christian theologian Karen Teel for a series on religion and death. Yancy noted that physicist Stephen Hawking was skeptical about life after death. He called it "a fairy tale for people afraid of the dark."[11] Yancy asked Teel how she, as a Christian, would respond to the charge that Christians are simply "afraid of the dark."

Teel said that she had cared for her mother as she gradually lost her battle with ALS, a disease that had also claimed Hawking's life. The disease was relentless and cruel, she said. Her mother had been an accomplished pianist, but at the end her body had deteriorated to the place where Teel had to help her with everything: eating, using the bathroom, controlling her wheelchair, even breathing. But as she journeyed with her mother toward death, she found that in her sorrow, her own faith had been renewed. "Before facing my mother's death," she said, "I never really knew that I believed that life continues. . . . I know it as I know the sun will come up in the morning, as I know I'll get wet in the rain, as I know I love my own children. It isn't about fear. It's a gift and a mystery, this conviction that we come from love and we return to love."[12]

She had tears of grief, but in God's mercy, her tears had become bread.

Prayer for the Day

Feed us, O God, in your mercy. Feed us in days of joy and laughter, and feed us also in times of trouble and grief. In the name of the Christ who wept his own tears at Gethsemane. Amen.

Fourth Week of Advent

God's Affection for the Small

Micah 5:2–5a

And he shall be the one of peace.

—Micah 5:5a

The fear of insignificance is a very old human fear. We all want to make sense of our lives or find some satisfying story of meaning—a frame, if you will, that orders all the disorder and buffers the gnawing emptiness that arises for us individually and collectively. Most of us know in our bellies that fame, wealth, and achievement are only surrogates for the significance we seek. We long for those flashes of awareness that hint of something truer.

One of these numinous moments arises for a community in Micah 5 when God singles out and blesses little Bethlehem. At that time, Bethlehem was an easily overlooked community overshadowed by its past as King David's hometown. Their glory days were behind them and clinging to that bit of nostalgia seemed to be the sole bridge to significance. But no, in Micah 5:2, God cups Bethlehem's face, pinches her cheeks, and says, "But you, O Bethlehem of Ephrathah, who are one of the little clans of Judah, from you shall come forth for me one who is to rule in Israel, whose origin is from of old, from ancient days." Then and now, the words are a salve to all who feel a waning sense of significance. Bethlehem hears that she matters, that her smallness is not an obstacle or a shame, and that God will radiate new possibilities there.

The joy in this news is not all set in the future. Apparently, goodness, worth, and wonder already abounded. I imagine the notion that Grace had perched among that small circle of neighbors brought supernatural meaning to ordinary tasks. The routines that seemed to be of so little consequence proved to be bound up in the hidden will of God. Is this really any surprise? God has an affection for the small. Small towns like Bethlehem and Nazareth. Small people like David and Zacchaeus. Small gifts like the widow's mite or a boy-sized lunch of fish and bread or a newborn in a manger. In God's hands, the small have an inherent dignity and quiet majesty.

Advent urges us to see ourselves and the world through this divine gaze. This means shedding the fascination with grandeur and seeing our humble lives through the lens of the gospel—a lens that repeatedly redeems the small and unremarkable and refracts light through our shattered hopes. Cherishing the small means letting the facades of significance crumble and welcoming fresh visions of power. Cherishing the small means remembering the "homely and inconspicuous" roots of Christianity.[1] Few of our spiritual ancestors could grasp how pivotal their lives were in upending a distorted world. Our call is to trust the still, small voice that assures us we, too, are caught up in the Spirit's hidden and glorious work.

Prayer for the Day

Gracious God, in your hands tiny things flourish and contribute to a purpose beyond our knowing. Help us to entrust the whole of our lives to you, resting in the knowledge that in you alone we find our significance. Amen.

The Center Holds

Colossians 1:15–20

For in him all the fullness of God was pleased
to dwell, and through him God was pleased to
reconcile to himself all things.
                    —Colossians 1:19–20a

Early in William Butler Yeats's famous poem "The Second Coming" are these words:

Things fall apart; the centre cannot hold;
Mere anarchy is loosed upon the world.[2]

Yeats wrote his poem in 1919, just after the devastations and dislocations of World War I and in the aftermath of the terrible 1918 flu pandemic. But it was not only war and epidemic that prompted Yeats to say that "the centre cannot hold." Many sensed that human history itself was coming loose—old structures of authority weakening, frames of meaning breaking apart, opening a space for the possibility that "mere anarchy is loosed upon the world."

Not surprisingly, Yeats's dark poem is experiencing a revival in our own day, when the threats of terror and political upheaval abound, and the threat of pandemic has become all too real. "Amid a bevy of bad news and political upheaval," says the *Wall Street Journal,* "journalists, commentators and others are turning to W.B. Yeats's chilling 1919 poem . . . with unusual frequency."[3]

Why? The reason, of course, is the deepening apprehension that "the centre cannot hold." Oxford historian Roy Foster named the anxieties of our time: "There's a sense of insecurity, instability, risk, and a feeling that something appalling is around the corner."[4]

Paul's Letter to the Colossians was written in just such a time of anxiety and uncertainty. The world was under the oppression of Rome, the gods and goddesses of popular religion ruled life at whim, the church at Colossae was embroiled in controversy, and Paul himself was in prison. How could Paul encourage Christians in Colossae to have hope in such a world, a world in which it surely seemed that "the centre cannot hold"?

Paul does not display a false optimism, nor does he radiate superficial sunshine. He does not fabricate a rosy political analysis to predict an upbeat future. He knows the life of faith is a life of struggle. What does he do? He sings a hymn, a hymn to Christ. "All things have been created through Christ and for Christ," he sings, "and in Christ all things hold together" (Col. 1:16–17, au. paraphr.). This is a truth that only faith can see, a truth that allows people of faith to take one more step, to live one more day, a truth not argued but sung: in Christ the center holds.

An episode of the television series *The Crown* told the tragic story of the 1966 coal mine disaster in the Welsh village of Aberfan in which many schoolchildren were killed. Queen Elizabeth refused to go to the funeral but sent Prince Philip instead. In a moving scene, the prince stands with the villagers before an open grave holding scores of children's coffins. He weeps as the villagers, mourning the deaths of their own children, sing the hymn "Jesus, Lover of My Soul."

When Philip returns to Buckingham Palace, the queen asks him about the funeral.

"Eighty-one children were buried today," he tells her. "The rage . . . in all the faces, behind all the eyes. They didn't smash things up. They didn't fight in the streets."

"What did they do?" the queen asks.

"They sang. The whole community. The most astonishing thing I ever heard."[5]

Even in their grief, they sang. Even as their lives were shaken, they sang. In faith and hope, they sang that in Christ the center holds.

Prayer for the Day

Give us, O God, the eyes to see what only faith can see, that all things are held together in your Son, and then give us the hearts and voices to sing our faith and our hope. Amen.

The Right Words

Romans 8:18–30

> Likewise the Spirit helps us in our weakness; for we do not know how to pray as we ought, but that very Spirit intercedes with sighs too deep for words.
>
> —Romans 8:26

Have you ever been at a wedding or a funeral or a dinner with friends when someone opened with prayer and seemed to have just the right words for the occasion? The right words said in the right way can almost magically soften our hearts. We find ourselves saying things to God that we never knew we wanted to say. Somehow the prayer taps into a shared emotion or desire. This can happen in just a few words. Or even one. I have a friend whose eyes brighten whenever macaroni and cheese is on the table. With a quick nod and blink, he breaks into a beaming smile and says, "Aaaaaaa-MEN!" That's his table blessing: Amen. Yet it sings with gratitude.

Simple prayers with borrowed words carry us through the joys and difficulties of life. The Lord's Prayer. The

Twenty-Third Psalm. "Thank you." "Bless you." And, perhaps most of all, "Help me." These sacred words draw us into the stream of believers and doubters, living and dead, who have prayed the words and experienced an infusion of grace. And isn't it astonishing that when the church gathers for worship, tired words like "We pray for . . ." or "Lord, hear our prayer" can summon all the compassion in the room? Even if all we have is a first name or a first initial or fragments of a predicament, "We pray for . . ." is enough to swaddle the person with light and alleviate some element of the burden. We may not always know what to pray, but the Spirit finishes our sentences. The weakness that is so often an impediment to daily life creates no obstacle to prayer.

Then, there are the prayers composed with no words—only tears, sighs, groans, or sharp winces in restless limbs. The time comes when human weakness is unmasked, and words lose all usefulness. "Give heed to my sighing," the psalmist says, "Listen to the sound of my cry, my King and my God, for to you I pray" (Ps. 5:1b–2). "I think of God, and I moan; I meditate, and my spirit faints" (Ps. 77:3). "Because of my loud groaning my bones cling to my skin" (Ps. 102:5). And though in this life we may never understand why we suffer as we do, we are not helpless. The Spirit responds to our groans "with sighs too deep for words" (Rom. 8:26). This is our hope—that God sustains us in our weakness and does so in ways that surpass all human knowing—especially our own.

As a boy, Howard Thurman remembers suddenly bursting into a room and finding his mother kneeling in prayer.[6] When she turned to look at him, her face had a glow. She did not realize it, but it was as if she had been in the ether of prayer and somehow absorbed some of God's peace. And that is the miracle of prayer. To pray is to be enveloped in the tenderness of God, who carries us in our weakness.

Prayer for the Day

Gracious God, you are always near, always sustaining us, always doing more than we can imagine. Help us to entrust the whole of our lives to you, knowing that you hear every prayer. We pray in the name of Jesus, who intercedes for us in love. Amen.

Knocking Down Walls

Ephesians 2:11–22

So then you are no longer strangers and aliens,
but you are citizens with the saints and also
members of the household of God.
—Ephesians 2:19

You have to hand it to Jesus. When he decided to transform Saul into the apostle Paul, Jesus did not pick an easy
target. Saul was essentially a religious terrorist, one who
headed up the Damascus Road "breathing threats and
murder" against those "who belonged to the Way" (Acts
9:1–2). What so enraged Saul against the early Christians
was that, to his way of thinking, they were trying to knock
down a wall that must never be dismantled: the everlasting wall separating Jew from Gentile. Saul was willing to
risk his own life, and to take the lives of others, to keep
that wall standing.

But on the Damascus Road, Saul encountered a Jesus
who communicated to this seething zealot, "Come on,
Saul, Christians aren't trying to knock down the wall
between Jew and Gentile. *I* knocked it down, and I have

decided that you will cross over the rubble of this wall to become a missionary to the Gentiles."

Saul never got over that. The old hymn "Amazing Grace" announces "I once was blind but now I see," but that was not Saul's song. The heavenly light of the wall-destroying Jesus was so bright that for a brief time Saul lost his sight. "I once thought I could see, but now I'm blind" was, for a while, his hymn of grace. The experience of meeting the risen Jesus changed his name, changed his vocation, and changed his heart. Paul sings in Ephesians, "For [Jesus] is our peace; in his flesh he has made both groups into one and has broken down the dividing wall, that is, the hostility between us" (Eph. 2:14).

Walls can be the saddest of human structures. Whether they are built to wall people in or to wall people out, they are manifestations of our fears and our failures to live as God has created and called us to live.

"But we need walls," some will protest. "Where would we be without prison walls to keep us safe, or border walls to protect our national identity, or fortress walls to keep out the enemy?" Or, as the farmer in Robert Frost's poem "Mending Wall" says, "'Good fences make good neighbors.'"[7]

Perhaps, but we should remember it was the firebrand Saul, not the apostle Paul, who had the agenda of walls, and it was Jesus who interrupted Saul's mission of terror to tell him that the walls had been broken down and to proclaim peace to those far away and those near (Eph. 2:17).

It is the joy of those who belong to Christ to join him in taking down, stone by stone, the walls that divide human beings from each other—the walls that divide people because of race, the walls that divide men and women, the walls that separate rich and poor, and all other walls built out of hostility, self-centeredness, and fear.

As Paul discovered, the mission of peace and reconciliation is never simple or easy. Walls are easier to build than bridges, suspicion of others easier to sell than a vision of children at peace in the house of God (Eph. 2:19). But we travel now, not up the Damascus Road of rage and vengeance, but up the road of hope that leads to Bethlehem and to the Prince of Peace, and then beyond to the new Jerusalem, the city of God, where the gates of the city are never shut (Rev. 21:25).

Prayer for the Day

O God of peace, we praise you that in Christ you have torn down the wall of hostility and made us citizens with the saints and members of your household. Banish all of our fears and enable us to live as ambassadors of peace. Amen.

Slow Miracles

2 Peter 1:16–21

You will do well to be attentive to this as to a
lamp shining in a dark place, until the day dawns
and the morning star rises in your hearts.
                                        —2 Peter 1:19b

Twelve years after his historic release from prison, Nelson Mandela journeyed back to Robben Island where he had been confined. He wanted to take in the visual landscape that he had gazed at for so long—this time with artistic eyes. By drawing some of the dominant scenes, he hoped to tell a new story through them.

One of his more poignant drawings is a rendering of the prison lighthouse. Standing pale and lonely against a periwinkle sky, the lighthouse looks idyllic. The tones of blue and white lend an air of serenity to Mandela's scene, but is he depicting the serenity born of righteousness or the eerie calm of impervious evil? As it turns out, he felt both. "It is true that Robben Island was once a place of darkness, but out of that darkness has come a wonderful brightness, a light so powerful that it could not be hidden behind prison walls, held back by prison bars or hemmed in by the surrounding sea."[8] The courage and resolve of prisoners like Walter Sisulu, Robert Sobukwe, and Mandela transformed Robben Island. Now its lighthouse symbolizes the power of the human spirit.

Like yeast rising in dough, like a sweet aroma in a dank room, like light in dark places, we can change the atmosphere around us (Matt. 13:33; 2 Cor. 2:15; Matt. 5:14). The Spirit radiates love through us to expose wickedness for what it is and bring about true healing, but sometimes this process takes a long, long time. Few of us have the energy or the stamina for this slow work. We need companions, pep talks, promises, reminders, and examples. We need *faith*. Not the kind of faith that adds a little zest to an ordered life—like a lemon wedge in a nice glass of iced tea, but the kind of faith that can sustain us in the face of monstrous evil. Only supernatural insight can broaden our perspective on reality during the long periods when the work of transformation looks impossible. Neither cheap optimism or fantasy could sustain the hope of political prisoners as their beards and temples turned gray and their bodies grew thin from malnutrition. That took faith.

Such faith, sustained over years and decades, is a miracle in itself and as dramatic as the transfiguration or the feeding of the five thousand or the protection of Daniel in the lions' den. God's slow miracles may be even more dramatic given the mountains of despair and resistance that accumulate over time.

The author of Second Peter knows the pressures of life often wear us down, causing us to wonder whether we have been fooling ourselves by believing. No, Peter explains, "we did not follow cleverly devised myths when we made known to you the power and coming of our Lord Jesus Christ, but we had been eyewitnesses of his majesty" (1:16). "We have staked our lives on this faith," Peter seems to say, "and so can you." Our lives are anchored in the Living God who holds time and eternity. The Almighty One is working slow miracles through us.

Prayer for the Day

Hope of the Exile, Strength of the Freedom Fighter, work your mighty wonders through us. Give us the urgency to struggle for justice now and grant us the patience to wait without despair when we must. Heal, transform, and renew your world. We pray in the name of Jesus. Amen.

The Long Road to Bethlehem

Luke 2:1–14

> Joseph also went from the town of Nazareth in
> Galilee to Judea, to the city of David called Beth-
> lehem, because he was descended from the house
> and family of David. He went to be registered
> with Mary, to whom he was engaged and who
> was expecting a child.
>
> —Luke 2:4–5

It is roughly 100 miles from Nazareth to Bethlehem.[9]
According to Google Maps, it would take thirty-four
hours to travel it on foot, not counting stops for rest.
And, of course, Google does not factor in contingencies
such as marauding bandits, deep rain-washed wadis cut-
ting through the path, inns with no room, or full-term
pregnancies. But this long, wearying, unpredictable journey is, according to Luke, precisely what Joseph and
Mary undertake.

It is not as though they have a choice. This is no vaca-
tion jaunt to the old home place. Caesar Augustus has
spoken, and like it or not, everybody has to register in

the town of their ancestry. Joseph lives in Nazareth but has roots in Bethlehem, and that is that. Days and days of perilous travel ensue, Mary's water threatening to break at any minute, and the whole dangerous, exhausting journey is just to fill out some government forms. Compared to this, two hours spent languishing in the DMV waiting room seems hardly worth grumbling over.

For Luke, the question is where hope might be found for people like Mary and Joseph. They are, like poor and defenseless people everywhere and in every time, at the whim of whatever Caesar or mindless bureaucracy or uncaring machinery of state happens to lash out in their direction. Caesar issues a decree, drinks another glass of wine, eats a cluster of grapes, and Joseph and Mary pack provisions and head out on the Roman road to Judea. They are faceless nobodies under the boot of an uncaring empire. Their only hope—if they have any hope at all—is not in Caesar Augustus, but in the God of Israel, who accompanies them even when they walk through the valley of the shadow of death.

But we are not like Joseph and Mary, we say. We are children of a technological age, and we have said to ourselves, "Who needs hope? We have progress. By our own prowess and strength, things are getting better every day." But with economies faltering, the gap between rich and poor widening, glaciers melting and seas rising, pandemics raging, governments distant and unresponsive, we are increasingly disabused of the illusion that we need no hope beyond our own resources. We are now all Josephs and Marys, compelled by some distant Caesar or simply the crushing force of history to travel the weary road. But, by the grace of God, the road leads to Bethlehem, and a manger of surprising hope awaits us there. "We felt that we had received the sentence of death," writes Paul in 2 Corinthians, "so that we would rely not on ourselves but on God who raises the dead" (1:9).

Dietrich Bonhoeffer compares life in a prison cell to the hope of Advent: "One waits, hopes, does this, that, or the other—things that are really of no consequence—the door is shut and can only be opened *from the outside*."[10]

No longer confident of progress, no longer believing Caesar's empty promise of peace, maybe we are ready again for the hope and wonder of Bethlehem. Like Joseph, we are exhausted by the forced march of greedy empires, but like pregnant Mary, we suddenly realize that we have been carrying the true hope all along: God with us. Listen! Hear once again, sounding over Bethlehem, the angels' hopeful song of the only peace worth trusting.

Prayer for the Day

O God, we are traveling a weary road. The journey is long, and the dangers are many. Our only comfort is that even though we walk through the valley of the shadow, you are with us. Lead us, Good Shepherd, along the way, and take us at last to Bethlehem, where we may find our Savior and our hope. Amen.

Cosmic Rejoicing

John 1:1–14; Psalm 98

All the ends of the earth have seen
    the victory of our God.
                                    —Psalm 98:3b

A mystical cord binds the world together. Like gravity, it pulls with invisible but tremendous power. Many of us feel the cord during the Olympics or the World Cup, when athletes from all over the globe converge in one city, bringing the attention from their respective countries with them. And the cord sometimes sparkles with electric brightness. When New Year's comes around, we can watch the fireworks light up the night in Australia and then pass like a baton from Australia to Asia, from Asia to the Middle East and Africa and Europe. Hurdling across the Atlantic Ocean, the baton passes to North and South America for another sprint.

   Christmas brings us together, too, though often in more subtle ways. The birth of Christ reminds us that we are all God's children. And, as one human family, the walls that separate us feel harsher, whether they are visible walls of steel or invisible walls made of something stronger—like resentment or hatred.

Every year Yuri Kochiyama asked for stamps for Christmas and got testy with her family if she was given anything else. Yuri used the stamps to send letters to political prisoners all over the country. Once Yuri established a bond with someone, a stream of letters continually flowed and maintaining these friendships was paramount. She never wanted religious differences to become barriers, and even practiced Sunni Islam along with Christianity for a time because she was convinced God's compassion flowed through both.

Part of the urgency around the letters stemmed from the fact that she, too, had been locked away for a time and surrounded by barbed wire. As a young woman, Yuri spent two years in the Santa Anita Assembly Center in Jerome, Arkansas—an internment camp for people of Japanese descent during World War II.[11] She never forgot the humiliation of living in a converted horse stall, or the constant stench of manure, or the indignity of being incarcerated on the basis of race. She knew that even small gestures helped people claim their dignity under such circumstances. Letter-writing was a way of nurturing her friends' inner light and reminding them of their identities as children of God.

Christmas ought to remind us that we are all beloved children of God and held in the same affection as the Christ child. And, as we celebrate, hopefully we will all experience some of its unifying power. This, it seems, sits at the heart of its holiness as a season. The most precious gifts of Christmas are the shared gifts like joy and hope, and the precious words of the season are "all," "we," and "us." Isaiah says, "Unto *us* a child is born, unto us a son is given" (Isa. 9:6 KJV). The birth of Christ brought new meaning to the word "us."

Among those present to celebrate Jesus' birth were sheep and shepherds, choirs of angels, and glistening stars. Differences existed without becoming barriers and this joyous mingling reflects the bliss of heaven where cherubim and seraphim and elders encircle the throne along with four living creatures: "the first living creature like a lion, the second living creature like an ox, the third living creature with a face like a human face, and the fourth living creature like a flying eagle" (Rev. 4:7). Each heavenly being has individual beauty, but they glorify God together. The wonder intensifies as the circle expands. And, surely, the same is true for us.

Prayer for the Day

Holy God, you are our joy, our peace, our hope, our all. And you have blessed us with Jesus, the Light of the World. Hold us in his light, transfigure us in its glow, and make us conduits of his unfailing love. Amen.

Notes

Preface

1. Walter Brueggemann, "A Shape for Old Testament Theology," *Catholic Biblical Quarterly* 47, no. 1 (January 1985): 28–46.

First Week of Advent

1. Wendell Berry, "Leaving the Future Behind: A Letter to a Scientific Friend," in *The Art of Loading Brush: New Agrarian Writings* (Berkeley, CA: Counterpoint, 2017), 58.
2. Noah Adams, "The Inspiring Force of 'We Shall Overcome,'" heard on National Public Radio's *All Things Considered*, August 28, 2013, and archived at https://www.npr.org/2013/08/28/216482943/the -inspiring-force-of-we-shall-overcome.
3. Georges Bernanos, *The Diary of a Country Priest*, trans. Pamela Morris (New York: Macmillan, 1937; repr., Cambridge, MA: Da Capo Press, 2002), 53.
4. Harriet Powers (1837–1910) was enslaved as a child but quilted two major works. Her *Bible Quilt* is part of the permanent collection at the National Museum of American History and her *Pictorial Quilt* is part of the permanent collection at the Boston Museum of Fine Arts. Donyelle McCray, "Quilting the Sermon: Homiletical Insights from Harriet Powers," *Religions* 46, no. 9 (2018): 4.
5. Dietrich Bonhoeffer, "Who Am I?" in *Letters and Papers from Prison*, trans. Reginald Fuller, 3rd ed. (London: S.C.M. Press, 1967; New

York: Touchstone, 1997), 347–48. Citations refer to the Touchstone edition.

6. Judith Guest, *Ordinary People* (New York: Viking Press, 1976), 48.

7. Guest, *Ordinary People*, 50.

8. Bonhoeffer, "Who Am I?" 348.

9. Mary McLeod Bethune, "Last Will and Testament," n.d., https://www.cookman.edu/about_bcu/history/lastwill_testament.html.

10. Bethune, "Last Will."

Second Week of Advent

1. Catherine Clinton, *Harriet Tubman: The Road to Freedom* (Boston: Little, Brown, 2004), 102.

2. Testimony of Arnold Gragston in Ira Berlin, Marc Favreau, and Steven F. Miller, eds., *Remembering Slavery: African Americans Talk about Their Personal Experiences of Slavery and Emancipation* (New York: New Press, 1998), 68.

3. Tom Shales, "TV Preview," *Washington Post*, November 22, 1989, www.washingtonpost.com/archive/lifestyle/1989/11/22/tv-preview/bd787e2b-3b39-461f-bd64-eb46ef3cb5b9/.

4. Dana Greene, *Evelyn Underhill: Artist of the Infinite Life* (New York: Crossroad, 1990), 84–85.

5. Stephen Prothero, *American Jesus: How the Son of God Became a National Icon* (New York: Farrar, Straus and Giroux, 2003), 13.

6. Anne Lamott, *Bird by Bird: Some Instructions on Writing and Life* (New York: Anchor Books, 1995), 21.

7. Madeleine Delbrêl, *The Joy of Believing* (Sherbrooke, QC: Editions Paulines, 1993), 154.

8. "Bernice Johnson Reagon on Leading Freedom Songs during the Civil Rights Movement," interview by Terry Gross, *Fresh Air*, June 19, 2020, https://www.npr.org/2020/06/19/880245261/bernice-johnson-reagon-on-leading-freedom-songs-during-the-civil-rights-movement.

9. Elizabeth Landau, "Symphony of Stars: The Science of Stellar Sound Waves," Exoplanet Exploration, NASA Astrophysics Division, July 30, 2018, https://exoplanets.nasa.gov/news/1516/symphony-of-stars-the-science-of-stellar-sound-waves.

10. "Immigration," a resolution of the National Association of Evangelicals, 2009, https://www.nae.net/immigration-2009.

11. Robert Hayden, *Collected Poems*, ed. Frederick Glaysher (New York: Liveright, 1985), 41.

12. Julian of Norwich, *Revelations of Divine Love*, trans. Elizabeth Spearing (London: Penguin Books, 1998), 7.

Third Week of Advent

1. Rachel Carson, *The Sea Around Us* (1950; repr., New York: Oxford University Press, 1989), 69.

2. Carson, *The Sea*, 13.

3. Marty Haugen, "Gather Us In," copyright 1982, GIA Publications, Inc.

4. Jonathan Kozol, *Amazing Grace: The Lives of Children and the Conscience of a Nation* (New York: Crown Publishing, 1995), 268–69.

5. Saint John Climacus, *The Ladder of Divine Ascent*, trans. Colm Luibheid and Norman Russell (New York: Paulist Press, 1982).

6. Evelyn Underhill, *Advent with Evelyn Underhill*, ed. Christopher L. Webber (Harrisburg, PA: Morehouse, 2006), 61.

7. Annie Dillard, *Holy the Firm* (New York: Harper and Row, 1977), 57.

8. Pope Francis, "Pope at Urbi et Orbi: Full Text of His Meditation," *Vatican News*, March 27, 2020, https://www.vaticannews.va/en/pope/news/2020-03/urbi-et-orbi-pope-coronavirus-prayer-blessing.html.

9. Pope Francis, "Pope at Urbi."

10. Pope Francis, "Pope at Urbi."

11. Ian Simple, "Stephen Hawking: 'There Is No Heaven; It's a Fairy Story,'" *Guardian*, May 15, 2011, https://www.theguardian.com/science/2011/may/15/stephen-hawking-interview-there-is-no-heaven.

12. George Yancy, "'I Believed That I Would See Her Again': A Christian Theologian Recounts How Her Mother's Death Affirmed Her Faith and Belief in the Afterlife," *New York Times*, May 20, 2020, https://www.nytimes.com/2020/05/20/opinion/christianity-death-afterlife.html.

Fourth Week of Advent

1. Evelyn Underhill, *Advent with Evelyn Underhill*, ed. Christopher L. Webber (Harrisburg, PA: Morehouse, 2006), 67.

2. W. B. Yeats, *The Collected Poems of W. B. Yeats* (London: Wordsworth, 1994), 159.

3. Ed Ballard, "Terror, Brexit and U.S. Election Have Made 2016 the Year of Yeats," *Wall Street Journal*, August 26, 2016.

4. Ballard, "Terror, Brexit."

5. *The Crown*, season 3, episode 3, "Aberfan," directed by Benjamin Caron, written by Peter Morgan, featuring Olivia Colman, Tobias Menzies, Helena Bonham Carter, aired November 1, 2019, on Netflix.

6. Howard Thurman, *With Head and Heart: The Autobiography of Howard Thurman* (New York: Harcourt Brace Jovanovich, 1979), 15.

7. Robert Frost, "Mending Wall," in *The Poetry of Robert Frost: Collected Poems* (New York: Henry Holt, 1979), 33.

8. Nelson Mandela, *Motivation* (handwritten note introducing the Robben Island drawings), Belgravia Gallery, Surrey, UK, 2003.

9. A version of this devotion appeared as Thomas G. Long, "Living by the Word: Nativity, December 24 and 25, 2014: Luke 2:1–14 (15–20)," *Christian Century* 131, no. 25 (December 11, 2014): 21 and is used by permission.

10. Dietrich Bonhoeffer, *Letters and Papers from Prison*, 3rd ed., trans. Reginald Fuller (London: S.C.M. Press, 1967; New York: Touchstone, 1997), 135. Citations refer to the Touchstone edition.

11. Grace Gao, "Setting the Captives Free: Yuri Kochiyama and Her Lifelong Fight against Unjust Imprisonment," in *Can I Get a Witness? Thirteen Peacemakers, Community Builders, and Agitators for Faith and Justice*, ed. Charles Marsh, Shea Tuttle, and Daniel P. Rhodes (Grand Rapids: Eerdmans, 2019), 64, 66.

Made in the USA
Monee, IL
23 November 2021

82887839R00066